FREETHINKER

Rebuttal Poems

Book 2

By

Karima J. "K2" Sphere
KARIMASPHERE.COM

A Karima C. Johnson Entertainment, First Edition

Copyright © 2016 by Karima J. Sphere

Published in the United States by Karima C. Johnson Entertainment.

Karima C. Johnson Entertainment

Po Box 7767, Van Nuys, CA. 91406

Library of Congress Cataloging-in-Publication Data

Sphere, Karima J.

[Poems, Selection]

Freethinker: Rebuttal Poems

ISBN 978-0-692-71912-1

ISBN 10: 0-692-71912-1

Book design by Karima J. Sphere

Manufactured in the United States of America
10 9 8 7 6 5 4 3 2 1

Dedicated to the freethinkers whose perspective of the world enlightened mine.

Professor Curt Raney,
St. Mary's College of Maryland

&

David "Butch" Frazier,
Baltimore, Maryland

CONTENTS

Acknowledgement

Welcome to **FREE THINKER: Rebuttal Poems (book 2)** follow-up book to **Free Runner: Poems in the Wind (book 1). Free Thinker** is a collection of poems based on conflict between being a "Free Thinker" and seeing too many strive to assimilate into the status quo. I am grateful for my friends and colleagues who have encouraged me directly and indirectly to start this work, persevere, and publish it.

First and foremost, I want to thank GOD and His Will for allowing me the words to express my thoughts and feelings and the opportunity to capture them on paper.

I would like to acknowledge with gratitude, the love and support of my family, friends, and colleagues - Jeanette Johnson, Charles E. Jones, Al-Tron L. Jones, Kiisha Arnett, Neal Brown, Sr., Bertha Kenlaw, Anthony Hill, Kam Williams, Ricky Stewart, Pernell Marsh, Adrian Zeigler, Dana McGuire, Cicely Crosby, "Thee Family," and Cassandra Black (copy editor).

I am grateful to the professors at St. Mary's College of Maryland, Poet Laureate/Professor Lucille Clifton, Professor Michael Glasier, and Professor Curt Rancy.

I would like to express appreciation for my organizations - Organization of Black Screenwriters (OBS), and my fraternity Phi Beta Sigma Fraternity, Inc.

All proceeds from *Free Thinker: Rebuttal Poems* will help fund future projects. I hope you enjoy this book.

"A liberal is someone who thinks he knows more about your experience than you do."

— James Baldwin

The Rebuttal

My Poems
      My Poems
My Poems come at you like, …
Hardcore,
Parkour,
On all fours…
      Nah, better than that…

My Poems
      My Poems
My Poems come at you like, …
Security,
Got security,
Got security…
      Nah, nah, better than that…

My Poems
      My Poems
My Poems are Hip-Hop incarnate,
Make you vomit spit
"Oh Shhh...(it)"
Slip of the tongue—
Makes women come—faster
Oh hit you with a combo
Bigger than a Mayweather combo
Oh hit you with a combo
Five star blows
You never seen that gun, Yo.
I spit a verse
That leaves simple minds shook
No need for a hook here
Cause my energy penetrates sound waves
Causing you to be caught up in the rapture.

Laughter is harder to capture than pain.
This is something for the brain
From head to feet
     From head to feet
You can kiss my con-verse
Cause the police can't catch this.
This is white collar crime
Unlike the common cold catching ignorant fools slipping
I am clean as kept clean
While you are like a dollar
Falling out your back pocket,
You a lost one,
And you can't pay attention.

My Poems
     My Poems
My Poems come at you like, …
Security,
Got security,
Got security…
Like the 1932 movie Scarface son!
The black and white version of the sun, son
Hanging lonely in a moonlit sky, sun
And God's eye is bigger than the sky's sum
Life is beautiful, don't be the shy one.
Too much life to live,
To stay in the bed
And die of SIDS,
 Waking up son.

My Poems
     My Poems
My Poems come at you like, …
Hardcore,
Parkour,

On all fours…
I am a friendly person
Not a nice person…
        A friendly person
            Not a nice person
The only thing nice about me,
Is these FINE verses
Don't get it twisted
Like words I twist,
Around these VINE verses
Cause I make the grape,
The seed,
And the oil.

My Poems
        My Poems
My Poems come at you like, …
Like hands
In a honey pot
Making a fist
You stuck
Winnie Poohie-in
Cartoon-in
You out of place
You're ah, "Lemongrab"
And this ain't Adventure Time.

Antithesis: Subtitled Rougher
Dedicated to Chuck Maddox (Thee Family)

Antithesis
I nemesis my own synthesis
Synthesis a nemesis
Mind Trickery
Fuckery
Like that ego in Guy Ritchie's "Revolver."
Revolving like Bakugan
And some want Baraka to be gone
But they don't know how hard his job is…
Nor do they want it
But I will give it to you
Villainous Hero or Heroic Villain
You decide.

Biblically speaking,
I am Naomi if Ruth had changed her mind.
I became ruthless.
In a relentless world of unfair,
You want me to play fair.
"You out your rabid mind."
Like a dude carrying a bag of squirrels…

> *"Watch out for the Big Squirrels*
> *Watch out for the Big Squirrels*
> *Big Squirrels*
> *Big Squirrels*
> *Watch out for the Big Squirrels*
> *Watch out for the Big Squirrels."*

Remixed…Mixed up
Shock like season salt on food
It's the sweet with the sour
It's the bitter with the power
And you thought I was kidding like kids' do
Part Angel, Part Predacon
Bump those Autobots and Decepticons
They all on the CON
Like the Democrats and the Republicons
They shut the government down…while we suffered
Went on vacation…while we suffered
Gave themselves a raise…while we suffered
All of this is part of the Rougher.

Unfair
Fairly unfair
Is the American Dream
When most have to fail
For the few to succeed
The youth believe it will be me who succeeds
Cause that bum on the streets… "That ain't me."
But that music video rapper… "Yeah that's me."
And that work ethic is… "What, psssh, please."
That's when pipe dreams become pipe bombs
Cause you were never given instructions to build it right.
"Plausible Deniability"
Yeah right…

It's your fault, …It's your fault
Playing Hot Potato
As the world remains blameless
Like memories after a smoke high
I wake feeling injured but don't know why

Out of sight is never out of mind
Circumstances set you here
And to not care, "Amazes me"
Forgettable to this pop culture present…
"Amazes me"
Telling me it's common sense…
"Amazes me"
Sense ain't common
Just look at the world
Antithesis

Heavy

Dedicated to Femi the DriFish (5th L)

Hardhats must be worn past this point…

Heavy
I've known wisdom
And not spoke it
Sound and choked it
Like a choke sandwich
Going down
Somewhere between
A prefix vision of life
And a sulfur fix…
On how bad life can smell
When a fart lands in your pants heavy
The poetic word was so heavy
That my walk was funny
In my belly words revolted with ghetto meals
Hot dogs and beans
Nothing seems what it means
"I wasn't suicidal, but I was ready to go."
Like everything that was rewritten or bitten
Push button distractions became fatal attractions
Like Carnival rides
And brand name abstractions
Left my "I" naked
And my "Karma" cold,
From the separation.
Maybe they will like me more if I cut my hair
And yet do I dare to live out loud
Daring to stare into the abyss of the whispers
'Cause it is a chance I could get spit on.
Transformed by my rightful place in this
Solar system

You might now get pissed on
If you standing where I'm pissing
Blinded by times of thirst
I've reached points where I wanted to sleep myself
Into a coma
Away across the hall from "Good Times,"
like Willona
Became a Loner
'Cause the only craziness I could deal with was my own
"So don't sweat me while I got my shades on."
Hided dangers like inward sins
Roman 7: 21...

> *So I find this law at work:*
> *Although I want to do good,*
> *evil is right there with me.*

Hoping like the DriFish said,
"The end would justify the painful beginning."
And then again...
Falling short of God's splendor
All Glory is given to all God Almighty
And all the mistakes are my own.

Haiku- GOD

GOD, YOU ARE THE TREES

I AM THE LEAVES, AND THROUGH YOU

I AM BEAU-TI-FUL

Out Here in the Wilderness

Stand back two hundred feet son!
Windshields can't save you
My words hit harder,
Than Santa Ana **winds**
They earth **bends**
Like **earthquakes**
Waking you from your **slumber**
Lumber is what I'm caring
Out here in the wilderness.
        Timber!

Life wants to swaddle you,
But it doesn't have any good intentions
Like new born mommas.
It **wants to** pacify your movements
Wants to match your outfit **with its** purse
Bundle you up **with its** accessories
But you can't live like that.
You gotta bust **out**
Break **out**
Like a three-year-old with new legs
You gotta move
Run hard, **Run** fast
Past the lumbering giants
Past the interference of obstacles
Past this thought of "**not enough**"
        Timber!

You gotta do what I witnessed in Solvang
Little Tommy jumps off a curb
Almost gets hit by a teenager on bike
Mom says, "Boy **you can't do that,**
You can't do that."

16

And he turns to his mom
And says… **"I gotta jump."**
"I swear I gotta jump."
It was **unexpected**
Unexpected like Guillermo Del Toro's Cronos
And it was **there**
It just **sat there**
Golden in your hands
Opportunity
You not knowing what to do with it.
And **Opportunity** is missed by most
Because it is dressed in overalls and looks like work.
- Thomas Edison
This is **medicine** for you ailing spirit.
> Timber!

You want a **fair shake** in this **world**
You gotta **take** in this **world**
Develop all three eyes
To triple beam in this **world.**
Develop your box cutter dreams
In this **world.**
The packaging is scared of you
The blade is held **tight** inside your belly
In the shape of a lightning bolt,
Nowhere near the edge of **sight**.
You gotta push forth through the plastic walls
Through the paperboard label
Into the **daylight**
Where vampires of this world burn
In your **sunlight**
Don't shake your head **"No"**
You know I am **right**.
> Timber!

The sheer thought of this is…
Words worth
Now **fan it** baby, **fan it**
Can't, **Can it**
Cause it's fresh.
Out from the underground
Like **beets**
Nourish **your life's force**
Thumping with **your life force**
Outward like Dre's **Beats**
Into back alley whispers…
>*Stop thinking of suicide because God made
>assholes **too** and they don't think of suicide.*

This is a love letter to **you**
Drenched in truth
You may be **always** outnumbered
And **always** outgunned
But you are never alone.
Out here in the Wilderness
> Timber!

K2 the Mountain

To that poetess

People claim that I'm **hiding**
I'm not **hiding**
You're not liste-**ning**
I write in camouflage
Too down to earth
Like snipers in tall grass
To hear the twigs, break,

"SNAP"

Oh snap!

"Oh **snap**, that boy Scientific got shot up!"
"What's a **Scientific**?"

Nothing **Terri-fic**
Just an **acid-ic critic** saying nothing.
I am **Riddick** in this pitch black
Lacking no vision in seeing you…

"Why don't you take your **cape** off,
When you run your **capers**
Out here in the streets.
Assimilating poetry into,
What can get the next finger **snap**."

I'm not saying, **"That's wack"**
But my heart does not beat like **yours**
So why should my poetry sound like **yours?**
"I'm more concerned about living **right**
In the **sight** of God's **memory**"
I'm not on that **Tomfoolery**
In my **school-ery**
Like some.
Blaspheming saying, "I'm a **clocker**."
"I'm no **clocker**"
I don't tic or **toc**
I'm more like a **watch**er

19

"Stop hiding, stop hiding, stop hiding yo' face
Stop hiding, stop hiding, 'Cause ain't no hiding place"

You do this to be famous
I do this to **breathe**
Honestly, I do this to **breathe**
This is my **the-ra-py**
The way I deal with world and **me.**
I have dreams like Daniel,
Frighte-ning,
Like **Light-ning**
Enlighte-ning, like the chest **tighte-ning**
"Air is precious"
You don't believe me... **Lose it.**
Let's see how fast you **lose it.**
Don't let that **cool** make you a **fool.**
Let your **choice** make you the **chosen**
I chose not to **recycle** any word
I heard another poet **recycle**
That's a vicious menstrual **cy-cle**
Making themselves **suspect** and **lia-ble**
For trying to be the next American **Idol**
Deflecting the **introspect**
The greatest thing a poet can **do**
Is write something that changes his own,
And the people's world **view.**
So fellow poets don't **bore me.**
Delight me with your **hones-ty**
Letting the people know
It's not all about the **applause**
What's your **cause** for being here?

"Stop hiding, stop hiding, stop hiding yo' face
Stop hiding, stop hiding, 'Cause ain't no hiding place"

I'm **Bou**-gie!
I'm **Ghe-tto**!
I'm **Boo-Ghetto**!
You can **call me**, what you want to **call me**
But you won't **call me**…bull-shit
You can **call me** "Mr. flag on the **play**"
Cause there is no kidding in my **play**
Nor Nursery **rhymes** in my **spine**
No **blind** leading the **blind**
Moreover, you do not read me like numbers
When I am counting on you to do your own
Mathe-**matics**
The world doesn't need more **addicts**
Looking for their next **fix**
It needs **acti-vist**
Looking to help **fix** this broken system
We need you to do more than just **exist.**
We need you to light fires to keep sheer thoughts warm,
The predators **away**,
And the lost ones from going **astray**
This is not lit to end up in an **ash tray**
But you don't hear me **though, -oh**
You hear me like 3-year-old **Mateo**
 "Linda Listen Listen Linda,"
"Honey you ain't listening to me Linda"
I can't get through to **you**
I guess I'm hiding in plain **view**
Like K2 the Mountain

    "Stop hiding, stop hiding, stop hiding yo' face
 Stop hiding, stop hiding, Cause ain't no hiding place"

Stop Wanting, You Trippin...
(Sequel to "Wanting to be Loved has got me Trippin.")

Stop, stop, stop, stop, stop!
Stop looking at my dick
And talk to me...
You ain't "Her"
And I ain't "Him"

As you search for security
On the foundation of securing the dick
I know that you ain't never love me
You were just looking
For an express bus ride outside this, bitch.
And if that's the only reason you desired me...
I guess even to you,
I am an Invisible Man...

See, what you see is the shade
Of a black man's cool pose
And I suppose that all you needed to see...
Caught you glancing for about a minute.
Deciding not to take a chance
Because my hat didn't match my shoes...

Lately men for you have been
A pre-fix for smacking that ass
And creaming those thighs
A men-ial duty
Or some sort of man-ual labor
Like changing the oil in your car every 3,000 miles
And I hoped we were doing
More than just flirting,
To fuck one another
Possibly exerting some time,
To know one another

22

Maybe just maybe earning,
To learn each other
And yet we aren't doing,
None of that…
We just fuckin' to relieve some daily stress…
And I guess that's how you were raised.
Or just how men have been fuckin you over.

"Wanting to be loved has got, you Trippin.'

The Dead, May 11th

"I understand you Gabriel Conroy."

I don't know you anymore
Trying to find a custom fit
In an off the rack world
What the hell do you want?

I do not fit in your frame anymore
My extremities fall away
Like dead branches,
From your acid rain fall
…And you kill me,
Claiming to know the world,
But, lost in the stew of things.

Your name does not fit here.
Your growth,
Your weeds, wrap
The air in my lungs
Spilling the sweet from my voice
The voice that used to say your name
And find joy in saying it.

You lost what many want,
Someone who wants you forever,
Forgotten, forever
I do not love.
I will not cry for the pain,
That has manifested in my heart
I only toast and drink to the strength
That comes from the rain
…And that's why I drink by myself.

After her, Japan

M.

After her,

Ain't shit truly

Here for me and

I got the hint when

You became too busy to bother,

Phone rings stopped echoing in my ear

And you no longer cared about watching sunsets

Wish I could invert this truth into homegrown sunrises

From inside our dance; having fits of laughter

Inside our spirits, a flash of tickle

A hope to cultivate blossoms on

An incline with legs strong,

Footing correct in place,

Lungs breathing big,

And smiles

Ablaze.

July Twilight

July Twilight
Painted words come to me in dreams
But none are the shade of you
None feel right like soft sand under foot
With your hand,
In mine.

I dream of you in measures of music
A time signature of perfect timing
Between bar lines
Between the burden of the privileged
A note holding on to sound,
Of your voice.

I long for your notes singing in my ear
I just wanted to know you
In word, In definition
In mystic revelation
In everyday thought
In whole, like the moon above the earth.

Your spirit is a curvature of Space-time
Creating circular waves of life
That splashes upon remote shores
Unbroken, Never in part like a Miniseries
But in a greater radius than itself
In a timeless expansion of love.

Light falls on to Butterfly wings
Like my eyes fall upon your beauty
From ancient graces that make sunflowers cry
I see you in space before the capital building of my heart
I see you space after the extinction of words
Where humming your favorite tune feels right.

Oh baby, imagine that.

Hashtag 3AM, Me

#My hell

Is waking up in my drawers

Infomercial squealing in the background

Telling me, "If I want it, I can get it."

All the lights are ON.

Projects blaring on computer

Ideas piled on desk

When am I going to have time to finish all these ideas?

Don't nothing begin till I'm finished.

My phone is nowhere to be found

Where the hell is my phone?

Alarm whistles from the crevice of the futon

I squirm my arm into the narrow straits

Reaching, reaching. Ahh, almost there

And I still can't see what I'm doing

Damn, my watch is caught on something

Meanwhile the TV is watching me …

Mocking me

"If I want it, I can get it."

Stuck in my disgust

Misplaced too

I'm suppose'ta be sleep

Now waiting for the jaws of life to set me free

Hashtag 3am, me…

THE BEATNIK (2016)

Inspired by Baltimore Penn Station, Marc Train

"CHUGGA chugga chugga CHUGGA CHOO"
As the train hustled down the railway
In its speeding loco-commotion

Delaying loving thoughts
And touches of dears
And darlings,

Dropping tight suits off
Frustrated with the day
Into ignorantly cold train passageways

My mind breathed a sigh of relief...
"The day is finally over."
Tired of the status of "intern"

My mind wanders into an empty place
Where the mind just drifts
On time, places, and people...

"CLACKETY-clack Clackety-Clack CLACK"
"The 60's Years of Hope Days of Rage,"
Slid out from my satchel.

It was just a book to me that gathered dust
Like all the profound and ridiculous titles.
For an educated man to read...

Yet I found myself reading about...
"Allen Ginsberg."
"Allen, Ginsberg, How absurd?"

28

Allen Ginsberg in his time,
Was a white Bohemian broom story.
"Who, who, who... Howled!"

Who spoke from his siren of beat jazz
On top of mental concrete towers
His voice hung shadows across landscapes

He defined his season
Seducing the beat down
And yet...

When he came to my school
I didn't even go to his lecture
"Allen Ginsberg who?"

That fool didn't know about my struggle,
My grief ...watching the TV lusting for my woman
With everything except me.

I wasn't suppose'ta see her
I wasn't suppose'ta want her
As if I could never love her.

I was suppose'ta see only term papers
Which by the way were up to my ass,
And a "free ride" was the imagination of majority

This minority worked hard for mine.
At the same time,
Trying to live out the reason for a rhyme

And the question of the day
That persuaded me to think the way I think
Was pronounced like this...

"Let me as'k you this,
Let me as'k you this…
Can you whip, my ass?" (-Chris Rock)

"CHOO, choo, woo, WOO"
I had to become a taskmaster
'Cause there is no sunshine where I'm from

I, became a Hip-Hop mixtape
"Needing to kick something
That means something…" (Pharcyde)

A spoken word verse about freedom
Yet I was cursed too
Cursed to constantly have to explain myself…

I stitched myself into the invisible
Caught sail into the love of the light…
Baltimore gleamed in ecstasy's night

"And I know you will see the light…
Once you, Understand
What you, Mean to me, Dar-lin."
(-Pharaoh Monch)

"ZOOOSH ZOOOSH zooosh Ding DING DING"
I could not believe my mind lingered on him.
That cadence of "Cool, Cool, Allen Ginsberg cool."

Attacking "Calculating Thinking"
Snapping crazy fingers…
"I guess that's poetry."

It was on my Beat Movement,
It was on the craving for redemption
From the time we are living in

And I guess that is what made me think of him.
"Allen Ginsberg."
His name is a zipped file on the same disk drive

The engine huffed, puffed to a halt.
And as I exited the train at Penn Station
I could not believe, he…

Allen Ginsberg was on this train ride
From Washington, DC to Baltimore
Eating oatmeal cookies

Shedding crumbs on my leather exterior
Trying to make eye contact
Maybe, there is a lesson to be learned here

Someday,
Maybe when my life
Comes close to passing me by

I'll return to the same spot on the train
Where Allen Ginsberg hangs out
And see what he was saying…

"What is to give light must endure burning."

--Viktor E. Frankl

Glossary of Terms

A. The Rebuttal

1. Parkour- the sport of moving along a route, typically in a city, trying to get around or through various obstacles in the quickest and most efficient manner possible, as by jumping, climbing, or running

2. Lemongrab- The Earl of Lemongrab, Adventure time character, is the first being Princess Bubblegum ever created and lives in a realm also called Lemongrab. Lemongrab is socially dysfunctional, and has trouble interacting with Candy Kingdom citizens due to his intolerance towards anything happy or comical.

3. Adventure Time- is an American cartoon series for Cartoon Network. The series follows the adventures of a boy named Finn and his best friend and adoptive brother—a dog with the magical power to change shape and size at will.

B. Antithesis: Subtitled Rougher

1. Guy Ritchie- Guy Stuart Ritchie is an English filmmaker known for his crime films. He is well known for his films Lock, Stock, and Two Smoking Barrels, Revolver, and Sherlock Holmes. He was married to Madonna for eight years.

2. Revolver- is a 2005 crime thriller film co-written and directed by Guy Ritchie. The film centers on a revenge-seeking confidence trickster whose weapon is a universal formula that guarantees victory to its user, when applied to any game or confidence trick.

3. Bakugan- *Bakugan Battle Brawlers* is a Japanese-Canadian action adventure cartoon produced by TMS

Entertainment and Japan Vistec. The story centers on the lives of creatures called Bakugan and the battle brawlers who possess them.

4. Naomi- Biblical figure- Is the mother -in-law to Ruth. Both her husband and son were killed and Ruth decides to stay with her because of love.

5. Big Squirrels- A Chuck Maddox remake of the Baltimore Club song, "Watch out for the Big Girls."

6. Predacon- Usually depicted as antagonists in the fictional universes of the Transformers storyline. Usually, they have a relation to the Decepticons, the more prominent antagonists of the series.

7. Plausible Deniability- Is the ability for persons (typically senior officials in a formal or informal chain of command) to deny knowledge of or responsibility for any damnable actions committed by others because of a lack of evidence that can confirm their participation, even if they were personally involved in or at least willfully ignorant of the actions.

8. Hot Potato - Is a party game that involves players gathering in a circle and tossing a small object such as a beanbag or tennis ball to each other while music plays. The player who is holding the "hot potato" is out when the music stops.

C. Heavy

1. Chock sandwich- A peanut butter and jelly without anything around to drink to wash it down.

2. "I wasn't suicidal..."- Connected to poem Free Runner in book, "FREE RUNNER: Poems in the Wind."

D. Out Here in the Wilderness

1. Santa Ana Winds- Strong, extremely dry down-slope winds that originate inland and affect coastal Southern California.

2. Solvang- Danish for "sunny field" is a city in Santa Barbara County, California. It is located in the Santa Ynez Valley. It is known for its wine tasting.

3. Guillermo Del Toro- Acclaimed Mexican film director and screenwriter known for his films Hellboy, Cronos, and Crimson Peake as well as the Oscar- nominated Pan's Labyrinth.

4. Cronos- A 1993 Mexican vampire horror film written and directed by Guillermo del Toro. A mysterious device designed to provide its owner with eternal life resurfaces after four hundred years, leaving a trail of destruction in its path. *Cronos* is Guillermo Del Toro's first feature film.

E. K2 the Mountain

1. Scientific- A character in Spike Lee's Movie Clockers, Played by Sticky Fingaz.

2. Riddick- Played by actor Vin Diesel, is a fictional character and the antihero of four films in the Riddick Series

3. Stop hiding- Verses in Black Stars' song, "Thieves in the Night."

4. Daniel- Biblical figure who is the hero of the book of Daniel. He is taken into captivity by King Nebuchadnezzar of Babylon. He prophesied the destruction of Babylon.

5. Mateo – 3-year-old kid who is an internet star for arguing

with his mom.

6. K2 the Mountain- The second highest mountain in the world, after Mount Everest, at 8,611 meters (28,251 ft.) above sea level. It is located on the China-Pakistan borders between Baltistan.

7. Triple Beam- An instrument used to measure mass very precisely. This phrase also refers to a light beam or beam of light. It is a directional projection of light energy radiating from a light source.

F. Stop Wanting, you Trippin'
1. Invisible Man- A novel by Ralph Ellison about an African American man whose color renders him invisible, published in 1952.

G. The Dead, May 11th
1. Gabriel Conroy- Main character in the story The Dead. "**The Dead"** is the final short story in the 1914 collection Dubliners by James Joyce. He finds a profound affirmation of life in the story.

H. #3AM, Me
1. Hashtag- A type of label or metadata tag used on social network and microblogging services to make it easier for users to find messages with a specific theme. Hash character (or number sign) #

I. The Beatnik
1. Allen Ginsberg- An American poet and one of the leading figures of both the Beat Generation of the 1950s and the counterculture that soon would follow.

Biography

Karima J. "K2" Sphere (born Karima Chew Johnson, October 18, 1974) is a Poet, Screenwriter, Playwright, and Filmmaker. Sphere was born in Baltimore City, Maryland and has always had a unique way of seeing things, and through his writing, he shares his insight.

He received his high school diploma from Baltimore City College, third oldest high school in the nation. After graduating, he continued on to St. Mary's College of Maryland, Public Honors College. It is one of only two colleges with this designation in the United States.

In 1996, at St. Mary's College, Mr. Sphere got the multi-media creative itch. He is constantly finding ways of involving all elements of his artistic talent into every project. As Head Event Coordinator (college job) he wrote, directed, and produced a series of commercials promoting Spoken-Word Poetry at St. Mary's College. This event helped foster a relationship between St. Mary's College and the spoken word and slam poets of the DMV.

In 1998, after graduating with a degree in Political Science, Karima J. Sphere returned to Baltimore to help his family and to give back to his community. He became the first African-American Intern for AdCouncil. While at AdCouncil, Karima was the online voice for Smokey Bear, and worked on the Welfare-to-Work Program. He also helped form a Spoken Word Poetry Group, "Thee Family." Many consider Thee Family very reminiscent of the Last Poets. The Family toured, produced CD's, books, and had a large poetry following.

In 2001 after waking from a life-changing God dream, Sphere decided to move to Los Angeles to follow his dreams just fifteen days before 9/11. In 2004, he became a member of

OBS (Organization of Black Screenwriters). In 2005, Karima wrote, directed, and produced his first short film, *"Finding the Boom-Bap."* Finding the Boom-Bap is the metaphor for finding love through a perfect blend of Beat and Melody. "Finding the Boom-Bap" premiered at Oberhausen International Film Festival. In 2010, Karima wrote, and produced the Documentary Web Series, *"Web Series-Hollywood Stories."* This documentary is about the lives and the challenges of people living their dreams in Hollywood. To date, it has garnered over 42.8K downloads worldwide.

In 2014, Karima Sphere wrote and published his first Poetry Chapbook, *Freerunner Poems in the Wind,* under his own company, (KCJE) KARIMA C. JOHNSON ENTERTAINMENT. He also has written and co-produced projects for the 48-hour Film Festival and various festivals around the globe.

Currently, Sphere is in production for his Biblical Sci-fi short "Mark of Denim," co-producing his first play, "The Poindexters," and rewriting/directing his first horror feature, "Auction Day." Mr. Sphere is diligently working on completing all his artistic endeavors this year in order to focus his attention on Law School. For public speaking, press, and publicity inquiries visit KARIMASPHERE.COM.